WHERE I COME FROM

WRITTEN BY
ROMALITA HARRISON
ILLUSTRATED BY CAMERON WILSON

WHERE I COME FROM

Published by Lee's Press and Publishing Company
www.LeesPress.net

A Premiere Self-Publishing Services Company

All rights reserved 2024, except for brief excerpts for review purposes, no part of this book may be reproduced or used in any form without written permission from Romalita Harrison.

This document is published by Lee's Press and Publishing Company located in the United States of America. It is protected by the United States Copyright.

Act, all applicable state laws, and international copyright laws. The information in this document is accurate to the best of the ability of Romalita Harrison at the time of writing and artwork.
The content of this document is subject to change without notice.

ISBN-13: 979-8-9886270-8-1

DEDICATION

To my ancestors, for your strength and light.

To my grandparents, my mother, my precious daughters and my beloved husband.

To Dorothy Jean, Sheila, Yolanda, Melissa Fox, Rose Hudson-Hill and my teacher and mentor Joyce Anderson.

AUTHOR'S NOTE

"Where I Come From" is a heartfelt journey written for those who have ever felt the weight of discomfort when the topic of slavery arises—a narrative that invites readers into a space of empathy and understanding. As the story unfolds, it traces the path of the enslaved from the shores of Africa to the complex tapestry of American history.

Inspired by the poem, "Memories of a People", *Where I Come From* is a tribute to the enduring grace and strength that characterized the lives of those who faced the harsh realities of slavery.

Where I Come From is a solemn homage to the memory of those who never knew liberty; whose remarkable stories have been obscured by the shadow of their plight. It strives to unearth and honor their legacy, revealing the depth of their existence beyond the confines of their circumstances.

In an imaginative interpretation, this poetic narrative shares a message from the enslaved to children of today; dispelling the notion they were merely defined by their enslaved status. Instead, it emphasizes their humanity — real people with feelings, dreams, aspirations, and gifts that were tragically taken from them, and bestowed upon America.

Where I Come From seeks to dissolve any sense of shame associated with the contemplation of these lives. Rather, it encourages readers to see the best of who they were amid the most challenging circumstances. In doing so, it builds a historical bridge connecting us to a heritage that declares the enslaved were not just victims, but resilient people who through their strength empower us to recognize our shared inalienable presence as human beings made in the image of God.

WHERE I COME FROM

The vibrant green, and the golden yellow became smaller in the distance, as the ships sailed away from the great continent over the warm waters to a place beyond the sunset.

They were given new names and clothing that scratched
and restrained their beautiful bodies.
Here, in this new place the earth was hard
and the air was thick,
the words were flat and the food made them sick.

In this new land, there were tears and tears and tears
of how things fell apart.
Each morning was a prayer held together
by their whole hearts.

They learned to do new and difficult tasks in the sweltering sun...
in the pouring rain... for long hours; nothing here was the same.

They were intelligent and strong,
hard-working, and true.
Their fingerprints are visible in everything we do.

They were architects and carpenters and engineers too.
They built grand new homes, and exquisite churches anew
with steeples that reached up to touch the sky so blue.

They were artisans, brickmakers and bricklayers. They laid floors,
shingles and built staircases so grand.
They carved molding and made fine furniture,
with only the toil of their hands.

They built wagons and ships and sewed canvas for sails.
In the rough seas each held their course in the stormiest of gales.

They were veterinarians and animal trainers around the clock.
Horses, cows, pigs, were a few of the animals they tended,
among all the other livestock.

They were horticulturists and gardeners. They planted seeds and harvested crops. They used flowers and herbs for healing. They did it all; sunup to sundown with no time to stop.

They were midwives, nurses, and doulas. When others were ill they did what they could. They delivered newborn babies and cared for the sick and fever stricken when no one else would.

They were designers, seamstresses, quilters and tailors on call. They
made fashionable silk dresses and suits for promenades
of belles and gentlemen in great halls.

They were chefs, bakers, preserve makers and more.
Their talents far exceeded what they were often used for.

They were inventors, scientists, and chemists.
There were so many jobs they learned.
Some big, some small.
They were teachers, poets, writers, musicians and orators.
There was no end. They gave it all.

There was no limit to what they had to give;
each one giving America something special
in the work they were forced to do.
They did the work for hundreds of years
Their story is our story, even their tears.

Their hearts beat in a different space and distant place.
Their triumph lives on through their amazing grace.

The winds of the same air blows
through generations to find us,
to comfort, to teach us what's true;
that we have always been loved by God
no matter what anyone tries to do.
They tell us, their stories are our stories too.
Ours to embrace and hold close
in the new things we choose to do.

They share their lives as gifts
worthy of remembrance.
Their stories are our strength
a beacon of light to see our future independence.

We remember
the shores of where we came from...

To shine for all time.
To guide us through
to a new dawn filled with the golden wonder
of their courage, forgiveness and love;
crafted from the heavens in the words of our very own song.
They wanted us to know
They were not only just the enslaved.
There was so much much much more that they gave and gave and gave.

They were smiles
and laughter
and minds that
dreamed dreams
of running wild and dancing in the moonlight
chasing the stardust of liberty.

They would want us to know;
They climbed mountains.
Their lives were not mere dust.
They would want us to know where we come from.
We carry their light
and the beauty of who they were
lives on in us.

My Family Tree

MEMORIES OF A PEOPLE

Our eyes forever hold
the photographic negative
of the ships that came
like a pestilence in the night;
canvas whipping like
black capes in a tempest storm.
We stood in the silence,
helpless and numb
to the true meaning of the moment.
We watched the millennium
of them sail away
into the midnight of the unknown,
a trail of crimson lay adrift
in the swell of the sea,
carrying the winds of a glorious aria
billowing the cadence and blue scent
of the beautiful bodies
gone past the horizon
where the tide drops away.
Their ghosts hover ever near to us,
their wails toll in the hills.
Tears that bear the names
of lives lost fill our buckets,
with the sorrow of a people
wrapped around & tethered in time
to the sacred precious memories
that linger in our minds.

PORTRAITS OF A PEOPLE

The following portraits are of real people who performed many of the jobs shared within the pages of Where I Come From.

Visit your local library or www.WhereIComeFrom.com
to learn more about their inspirational lives.

PORTRAITS OF A PEOPLE

Henry Boyd (1802-1886)
Henry Boyd was born on a Kentucky plantation. Early in life it was known Henry had a talent for carpentry. He started his own successful company that grew to include several buildings and factories. In 1844, he designed the "Boyd Bedstead," a bed frame that made beds more sturdy. His company made over 1000 beds. Henry also helped numerous people escape to freedom.

Bridget "Biddy" Mason (1818-1891)
Biddy Mason worked as a midwife and saved her money and used it to purchase land. Her estimated worth was $3 million dollars. Biddy was known for her kindness and generosity to help the poor. She founded a school for children and organized the first African-American Methodist Episcopal Church in Los Angeles, California.

Horace "The Bridge Builder" King (1807-1885)
Horace King was an African-American architect, engineer, and a highly accomplished and successful bridge builder in Alabama and across the south. He was also one of the wealthiest African-Americans in Alabama. His talent can be seen today in the three story spiral staircase at the state capital in Montgomery, Alabama.

PORTRAITS OF A PEOPLE

Susie King Taylor
Susie Taylor was the first African-American nurse during the American Civil War. She was the first African-American woman to publish her memoirs of her experience during the war. She was also an educator and opened a school for African-American children.

James McCune Smith (1813-1865)
James McCune Smith was the first African-American to earn a medical degree. He opened a medical office and a pharmacy. He became a powerful orator, writer, and a leading abolitionist and anti-slavery organizer.

Hercules "Uncle Hark" Posey (1748-1812)
Hercules Posey was an enslaved "culinary artiste" owned by George Washington. He served as chief cook at George Washington's mansion Mount Vernon.

PORTRAITS OF A PEOPLE

Sarah Marinda "Miss Doc" Loguen (1850-1933) was an American physician and pediatrician. Sarah was the daughter of Jermain Wesley Loguen, a noted abolitionist who had escaped slavery, and his wife Caroline. She was born the fifth of eight children at her family home in Syracuse, New York. Growing up her home was an important stop on the Underground Railroad. From an early age Sarah was interested in helping others. She received medical training and learned healing techniques from her parents and nearby Native American women. At 23, Sarah was admitted to Syracuse University School of Medicine. When she graduated from the Syracuse University College of Medicine she became the fourth Black woman in the United States to earn a formal medical degree.

Henry Kirklin (1858-1938)
Henry Kirkland was a prize-winning gardener and horticulturist and a successful businessman. Henry was the first African-American instructor at the University of Missouri. He achieved international fame for his work in horticulture and was known as "one of the best-known plant authorities of his era."

PORTRAITS OF A PEOPLE

Elizabeth Hobbs Keckley (1818-1907)
Elizabeth Keckley was born in Dinwiddie County, Virginia. She was renowned as a modiste (dressmaker) and seamstress. She was a keen businesswoman and used her earnings as a seamstress to purchase her freedom. Elizabeth's work as a dressmaker attracted the country's most elite women of the time to make their gowns and dresses. She became Abraham Lincoln's wife, First Lady Mary Todd Lincoln's personal dressmaker and companion. While in the White House, Elizabeth organized programs to support the former enslaved. In 1889 she published her autobiography, *Behind the Scenes*.

Nobert Rillieux (1806-1894)
Norbert Rillieux was born in New Orleans. Norbert Rillieux revolutionized the sugar industry by inventing a sugar refining process that reduced the production cost and provided a superior quality of sugar that is still in use today. The system is also used for soap, gelatin, condensed milk and glue.

Amanda Smith (1837-1915)
Amanda Berry Smith, a preacher and missionary, was born in Long Green, Maryland. She became a popular speaker in many churches and camp meetings. She was an inspiration to thousands of women. She funded The Amanda Smith Orphanage and Industrial Home for African American children.

PORTRAITS OF A PEOPLE

Ansel Williamson (1810-1881)
Ansel Williamson was born in Virginia. He was an American thoroughbred horse racing trainer. He is known for having trained Aristides, the winner of the very first Kentucky Derby in 1875. The Kentucky Derby is a horse race that is held annually in Louisville, Kentucky. That same year, his horse Calvin won the Belmont Stakes held in New York State. Ansel Williamson trained and conditioned dozens of other well-known horses who won other major races. His excellent horsemanship was known throughout the south. He is a member of the National Museum of Racing and Hall of Fame.

Harriet Powers (1837-1910)
Harriet Powers was one of the best known African-American quiltmakers. One of her first and most famous quilts is the "Bible Quilt." Two of her quilts are still in existence today, and they are the finest examples of the southern American quilting tradition. The quilts can be seen in the Smithsonian Institution and in the Museum of Fine Arts in Boston.

Vocabulary Matters!

Every person's vocabulary is unique.
It is important to explain what words mean
to children with child friendly definitions.
Vocabulary is key to reading comprehension.

Readers can't fully understand the story without
knowing the meaning of the words within the text.

Defining a word supports a child's understanding
of the story while also teaching them new words.

Children with a rich vocabulary tend to communicate
more effectively and have more academic success.

GLOSSARY

Architect
1. a person who designs (draws pictures of) buildings.

Beacon
1. a signal of light that guides or warns.

Canvas
1. heavy, strong cloth made of cotton or linen fabric.

Chemist
1. a person who conducts experiments in a laboratory (a place where scientists work).

Continent
1. one of the seven great divisions of land on the globe.

Designer
1. a person who makes or draws plans for creating something.

Distance
1. the measure of space between things, places, or points in time.
2. a place far away.

Doula
1. a woman trained to give support throughout the process of childbirth.

Gale
1. a very strong wind.

GLOSSARY

Horticulturist
1. a person who studies growing vegetables, flowers, fruits, or plants.

Independence
1. freedom from outside control.

Livestock
1. cows, horses, sheep, or other animals raised or kept on a farm or ranch.

Midwife
1. a person who is trained to assist women during childbirth.

Orator
1. a person who delivers a public speech.

Restrained
1. to hold back or control.
2. to take away the freedom of

Shingle
1. a thin, flat piece of wood or other building material. Shingles are attached in overlapping rows to cover the roof or sides of a building.

Shore
1. the land beside an ocean, sea, lake, or river.

GLOSSARY

Stardust
1. shiny pieces of cosmic dust found among the stars.

Sweltering
1. extremely hot, or very warm and humid.

Toil
1. long or difficult work.

Triumph
1. the winning of a great victory or success.

Veterinarian
1. a doctor for animals.

Vibrant
1. full of energy
2. colorful or bright

ABOUT THE AUTHOR

Romalita, a native of Newark, New Jersey, is a multifaceted individual with a passion for writing, spirituality, and community service. She is the creative mind behind "Conversations in Lavender," a poignant collection of prayers and poetry that speaks to the soul.

With a background as a chaplain and a former high school history teacher, Romalita brings a unique blend of wisdom and compassion to her work. Her journey in academia includes graduating from Duke Divinity School, where she specialized in Black Church Studies, and obtaining certifications in Youth and Theology from Princeton University Institute for Youth Ministry.

As an alumna of the esteemed HBCU Morris College and a proud member of Alpha Kappa Alpha Sorority Inc., Romalita is deeply committed to community leadership. She founded the Rockingham County Leadership Ambassador Program for young women and chairs Rockingham County Reads: One County, One Book, demonstrating her dedication to empowering others and fostering a love for learning.

In her leisure time, Romalita finds joy in simple pleasures, from reading to children and immersing herself in history to indulging in classic films and savoring lemon-flavored treats. She finds solace in rainy days, takes delight in the fragrance of gardenias, and finds inspiration in the breathtaking sunsets of autumn.

Romalita's life is a testament to the power of faith, education, and service. Through her writing and community initiatives, she continues to uplift and inspire others, leaving a lasting impact on all who have the privilege of crossing paths with her.

www.ingramcontent.com/pod-product-compliance
Lightning Source LLC
Jackson TN
JSHW041957151224
75419JS00001B/2